Hapkido:

Past, Present & Future

by   Todd L. Miller

Hapkido: Past, Present & Future

Todd L. Miller

Fifth Estate Publishing, Blountsville, AL 35031

Cover Designed by Owais Mohammed

Printed on acid-free paper

Library of Congress Control No: 2019943856

ISBN: 9781936533749

Fifth Estate, 2019

Table of Contents

1. Acknowledgments:

I would first like to acknowledge and thank my wife Michelle who has always been my best friend and encourager through our thirty years of marriage and martial arts training. She has always inspired me to follow my heart.

Michelle and Todd Miller.

I would like to thank my parents Loren & Pat Miller, who instilled a love of family, laughter and hard work. Sis and Bro: your grit and self-determination are inspiring. Thank you my brother for getting me started in hapkido.

From left: Susie, Loren, Patricia, and Shannon Miller.

I would also like to thank my hapkido teacher, GM Lim Chae Kwan who has persevered through my endless questions about history and techniques for 22 years. GM Lim has also been very generous in his teaching. Teaching the high level techniques that most will not share!

GM Lim Chae Kwan.

I would also like to thank GM Chung Woo Duk. GM Chung is one of the most respected taekwondo grandmasters in Daegu, Korea. I am honored to call him my instructor.

GM Chung Woo Duk Taekwondo 9th Dan.

It is very important for me to give sincere thanks to GM Daniel (Un Hak) Jung, (NH Kicks Taekwondo & Family Fitness Center) for boosting my morale at a time when I needed it most! I am forever grateful Sir.

GM Daniel (Un Hak) Jung.

I would also like to thank my God for His salvation and many blessings throughout my life.

2. Foreword:

When we speak of the founding of Hapkido we begin to argue even more about this art as controversial as its origins and techniques. In the US mainly this question as to the founder is of the most relevant, where many of GM Ji Han Jae's students recognize the same as the founder of the art. Within my experience, research and fellowship with Masters in the country of origin of the art, opinions are divided as to the affirmation of who is the founder. Especially when this person, Ji Han Jae, makes films in Hong Kong, plays with Bruce Lee and is based in the most important country in the world (USA), all this gets a fantastic repercussion and the speeches and affirmations always tend to be endorsed in chorus by his followers. My purpose in this foreword is not to argue, but to cause reflection. I am perfectly able to discern the situation and be impartial, undeniably acknowledging the contribution of Ji Han Jae throughout the world. Personally, if you will allow me not to worry, I never bothered to be a student of the "best", most famous, best technique, but I also admire people who train seriously with several excellent teachers.

I mean that caring about some quality of your teacher is important, but not depending on it to protect, hide, or use his or her name to promote. What is being the best? What do you understand about the best? If you think your Master is the best, you are judging your Master and you are usually below him. How can you say that he is the best? How many real masters do you know or know in your life? How many did you get to talk to? Have you ever talked to a Master who is impartial and can see a far greater horizon than your academy or association? These would be interesting questions to think about for example about the Hapkido Foundation. I have heard many and looking more comprehensively I can say that the story is always bigger than we imagine, cultivate or experience in a limited space. I write all this to say that this is a book of a disciplined Master, ethical and passionate for his art, just following his "DO", in a territory predominantly dominated by practitioners and masters who know a piece of history.

Todd Miller gives us an account of his experience, bringing us all a bit more of the story. We will hardly be able to understand from this book the whole story, but it will certainly be valuable to those who sincerely seek understanding of the origins and development of hapkido.

GM Luiz Miele, Hapkido practitioner since 1976.

Brazil

GM Luiz Miele in Korea.

3. Introduction

In this introduction I will be talking about my experience in taekwondo, hapkido and kuhapdo/iaido. It is my feeling that this is my experience in martial arts training and should be included even though this book is primarily about hapkido.

My first interest in hapkido began when I was very young. I saw the first "Billy Jack" movie at the cinema and knew I wanted to learn this dynamic martial art. There were very few martial arts classes offered in central Maine in the early 1970's. It took fifteen years before I would realize my dream of studying the art of hapkido.

Tom Laughlin as Billy Jack.

I started my martial arts training at Hwang's School of Taekwondo in Dover, NH under Instructor Richard Perreault in the 1980's. The school was named after GM Hwang Sung Kwang. GM Hwang was one of only three people General Choi Hong Hi promoted to 9th Dan in ITF taekwondo. I have the highest respect for GM Hwang and his continuing the legacy of General Choi Hong Hi.

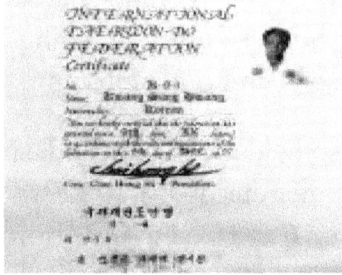

GM Hwang Kwang Sung K-9-1, ITF 9th Dan from General Choi Hong Hi.

I was training diligently in preparation for my 1st Dan test in ITF taekwondo when a hapkido master stationed at a local military base joined our school, his name: Master "Tall John" Kukowski. He started sharing hapkido techniques with the taekwondo students. Master Kukowski agreed to let me train privately with him. We began training as much as possible. The training sessions were tough and I learned a lot from Master Kukowski during this time!

Master John Kukowski seated on left with CM Todd & Michelle Miller.

I always will appreciate the concepts Master Kukowski taught me. One of the most important was to learn to fall safely. After several years of this training Master Kukowski was going to be transferred to another military base so he recommended I train with his instructor GM Mike Wollmershauser.

I made contact with GM Wollmershauser and began private lessons once per week. Soon I started attending his Thursday night class and took private lessons on Friday morning.

Master Mike also held the American Hapkido Association training camps each summer during the 1990's. I attended every one of these training camps on Cape Cod in my effort to learn all I could about hapkido. This was a very special time in my training as I learned a lot from Master Mike (this was what he liked to be called).

CM Todd Miller in Korea during Kuhapdo training.

In the mid 1990's a Korean grandmaster came to the USA to teach several hapkido seminars and I attended all of these seminars trying to learn the hapkido of Choi Young Sul! In 1997 I traveled to Korea for the first time with my wife Michelle and a group of students for the first summer camp in Daegu, Korea.

1997, 1st hapkido summer camp in Daegu, Instructors and students.

It was at this time that I met many of the direct students of Choi Young Sul. One of the most influential was Grandmaster Chae Hung Jun whose title is Hwe Jang Nim (most senior grandmaster). GM Chae was one of the few promoted by Choi Young Sul to 8th Dan in hapkido.

I remember training from 9:00 am-12:00 pm, our uniforms sweat soaked from the strenuous training, going back to our hotel to grab a dry uniform. We would go to the dojang for another 3 hours of training in the afternoon, get back to the hotel drenched in sweat and exhausted. This was difficult and rigorous training. It was also very rewarding to get to be on the mat with masters and grandmasters who trained directly with founder Choi.

First hapkido summer camp in Daegu Korea 1997 with members of the American Hapkido Association.

CM Todd Miller, Michelle Miller and others in Korea 1999. CM Miller practicing Iaido in Korea 2001.

GM Chae Hung Jun demonstrating Jin Mu Hapkido at 2008 Korean Hapkido demonstration in Daegu Korea.

I remember many occasions that GM Chae would walk by, grab me and put me into a very painful technique or give some help with a technique! GM Chae's specialty was sun sool (attacking first) and throwing techniques. GM Chae was always very kind and during my 2nd trip in 1999 he took us to eat Soon Doo Boo Jigae (Spicy soft tofu and seafood soup). This is still one of my favorite Korean meals to this day! GM Chae was very generous to me and would teach techniques whenever he had an opportunity.

GM Chae Hung Jun (GM Chae was one of the few promoted to 8th Dan By Choi Doju-Nim.)

The training in Korea was not like anything I had ever participated in before! The training was exceedingly difficult but also very interesting and important for me as my goal was always to learn the true hapkido of founder Choi Young Sul. This was another step toward that goal. This first trip initiated the yearly trips to Korea to train and learn all I could learn from these great Masters.

During this period in my training GM Lim Chae Kwan was my primary instructor as he was the Chief Master at the Korean hapkido school and in charge of the training camps. GM Lim and I developed a great friendship through our training together. We would go out after training for food and discussion together. We always ended up training more, sometimes into the middle of the night! Once while training in a Daegu park late at night, a police officer came by as he heard me tapping my hand and yelling very loudly in pain! He asked what was going on? GM Lim said this miguk (westerner) wants to learn hapkido. The police officer laughed and continued his rounds in the park. I trained for 11 years as a member of the Korean hapkido school and had many great experiences during my time studying in Korea.

GM Lim Chae Kwan and CM Todd Miller. This is when I first felt the techniques of Choi Young Sul from GM Lim Chae Kwan & GM Chae Hung Jun-1997 Korea.

In 2002, I was the first Non Korean to be promoted to 1st Dan in Kuhapdo (Korean Iaido).

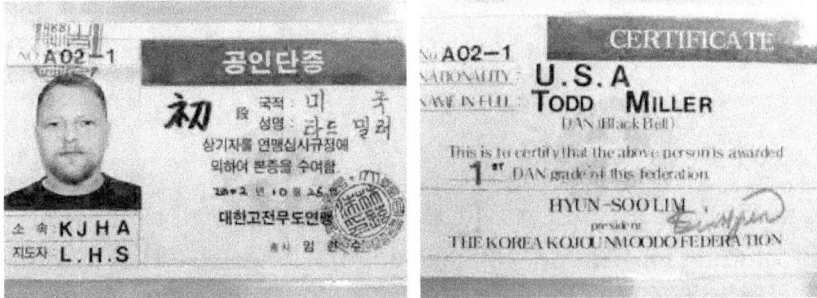

CM Todd Miller Kuhapdo certificate issued 2002.

I began training with GM Chung Woo Duk (Taekwondo 9th Dan) in 1996.

GM Chung Woo Duk, Taekwondo 9th Dan.

This training was with the World Taekwondo Federation. GM Chung was the top grandmaster in the Jido Kwan in Daegu. Under GM Chung's direction I tested and was promoted to 5th Dan black belt in taekwondo in 2002. GM Chung has students all over the world including GM Daniel Un hak Jung in Concord, NH. GM Jung was originally from the Daegu area in Korea. He has one of the best taekwondo programs in the USA that I have seen in my 30 years of martial arts! His students are great examples of excellent technique and more importantly courtesy, respect and humility.

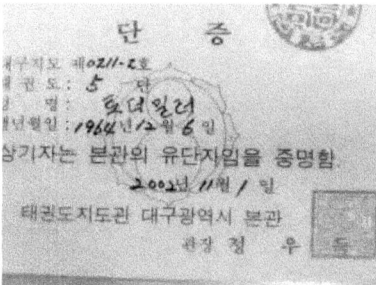

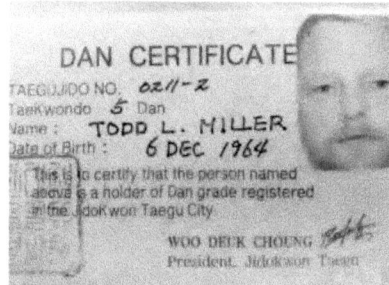

Taekwondo 5th Dan certificate, 2002. Master Todd Miller.

In 2007 GM Lim Chae Kwan, GM Chae Hung Jun and I resigned from the Korean hapkido school and opened the Jin Mu Kwan as we wanted to follow more closely Choi's authentic hapkido.

GM Lim Chae Kwan & CM Todd Miller in park outside of Daegu 2018.

GM Mike Wollmershauser, CM Todd Miller & GM Chung Woo Duk, 1998.

4. Hapkido

In order to describe what hapkido is, what I first need to do is talk about where hapkido came from. I will not go into the ancient history of hapkido but will focus on the more recent history. I will start with the modern day founder of hapkido Choi Young Sul. Choi spent 30 years in Japan and studied with one of Japan's greatest martial arts masters, Takeda Sokaku. This is why hapkido has similarities with modern day Aiki-Jujitsu, Aikido, Jujitsu and Judo but these similarities are very minimal. Hapkido is a very distinct and unique martial art with many techniques and principles.

Takeda Sokaku, Choi Doju-Nim's teacher for 30 years.

Hapkido is considered a soft style due to its non-resistance and circle principles by many, but in its softness it is very powerful. Some say that hapkido is the art of coordinated power but this definition does not really go deep enough in my opinion. Hapki literally means to harmonize or unite the energy/spirit, breath and physical body into one cohesive unit. Hapki also describes a type of internal energy and focus that very few masters know or at minimum don't teach! In Choi Doju-nim's hapkido there are three main principles that apply to all techniques. These three principles are Wha-harmony, Won-circle & Yu-flowing dynamic. It is these principles that give hapkido part of its uniqueness. Much study and meditation on these principles is essential to master the authentic martial art of hapkido.

Hapkido principles: Wha-Harmony, Won-Circle, Yu-Flowing dynamic.

Hapkido has gone through many different name changes since its founding. Originally it was called Yawara/Yu sool (soft technique). In 1951 it was called Dae Dong Ryu Hapki Yu Kwon Sool (Daito Ryu Aiki soft fist technique). Then in 1958 the term hapkido was first used.

The first Hapkido dojang sign attached outside Choi Young Sul's dojang in Daegu circa 1950's. Thank you GM Kim Jeong Yun for the historical picture.

There is some controversy about who actually first used the name hapkido but in all honesty the information I have found in my research is that Choi Young Sul was more concerned with the content of his art rather than what it was called! Choi referred to his art as hapkido later in his life. These days some use the earlier name hapki yu sool to distinguish their groups but most people use the name hapkido to describe the art. It is important to mention that Choi himself used the term hapkido on all of the certificates he issued as he was the Korea Hapkido President and founder of the art.

Some of the important masters in the early days of hapkido are Choi's first student in Korea, Master Suh Bok Sub. I met Master Suh in the mid 1990's and attended several of his oriental medicine in martial arts seminars. These seminars were very interesting and valuable training for me. Master Suh was very kind and animated.

Grandmaster Kim Yeong Jae needs to be mentioned as he was thought by many to be Choi's most skilled student and the first to be promoted to 8th Dan by Choi. GM Kim was also Choi's chief assistant during seminars and demonstrations. However GM Kim is relatively unknown outside of Korea!

GM Kim Yeong Jae. First 8th Dan promoted by founder Choi.

I also want to mention GM Chae Hung Jun who was a student of both GM Kim Yeong Jae and Choi Young Sul. GM Chae was also promoted to 8th Dan by Choi. GM Chae was with Choi day in and day out until Choi's death in 1986. Many hapkido practitioners trained under GM Kim Yeong Jae.

GM Chae Hung Jun, GM Kim Yeong Jae & GM Kim's brother.

GM Kim Yeong Jae's 8th Dan Certificate from Choi Doju-Nim. No. 1, The first 8th Dan given by Choi.

GM Chae Hung Jun awarding certificates 1970's.

Hwe Jung Nim Chae Hung Jun during Hapkido demonstration in Daegu.

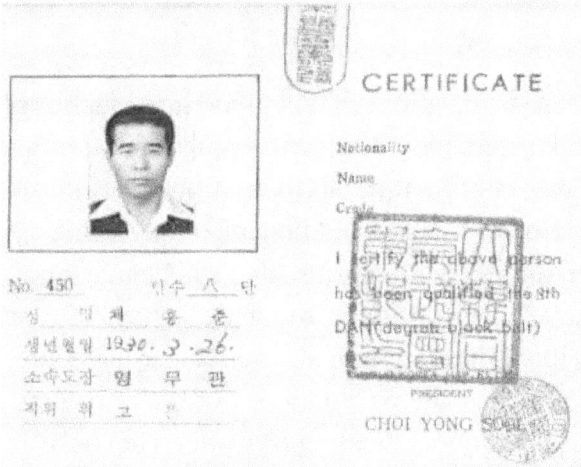

CERTIFICATE

Nationality

Name

Credit

I certify the above person has been qualified the 8th DAN(degree black belt)

PRESIDENT

CHOI YONG SOUL

No. 450

생년월일 1930. 3. 26.

GM Chae Hung Jun being awarded his 8th Dan by Choi Doju-Nim.

I also want to mention that there were 2 primary schools of hapkido, 1. The hapkido of founder Choi Young Sul with low kicking techniques and 2. the hapkido that has added high kicks & jumping kicks. Several Masters are credited with adding the high kicks. GM Kim Moo Hyung & GM Ji Han Jae, both were students under Founder Choi Young Sul for a short time during their youth.

GM Ji has done a lot to promote hapkido, acting in many Hong Kong movies, especially the famous Bruce Lee movie "Game of Death"! GM Ji has helped hapkido become well known in many countries around the world. GM Ji now teaches his Sin Moo system that he has developed over his many years in martial arts.

Bruce Lee & GM Ji Han Jae.

GM Ji Han Jae.

Now we see many different associations and hapkido organizations around the world. Some masters have started their own associations and have taken a number of important things away from Choi's Hapkido due to their lack of knowledge and understanding. One major thing that has been altered is the posture and stance that Choi taught. Many masters have added the deep and wide stances of other martial arts to hapkido. It is important to make very clear that Choi never taught deep or wide stances in his hapkido. Another mistake is that masters who lacked real understanding of Choi's Hapkido have added contradictory techniques! One example that is a common practice in many Hapkido schools doing multiple techniques one right after another! This is for demonstration only and has no practical value for self-defense! I would even add that this makes no sense as one technique if done properly is enough to finish the attacker's desire to fight any further.

Hapkido has much to offer for anyone seeking a complete martial art. Hapkido is first and foremost a fighting art, using low kicks to pressure points, strikes to pressure points and weak points, off-balancing techniques, body locking, breakaway, wrist, clothing, punch, knife, and weapons techniques. Hapkido has 3680 techniques according to founder Choi.

Many schools claim to teach hapkido today but hapkido has many differing interpretations and all are not the same! I think it is safe to say that most hapkido organizations teach the high kicking techniques that were added by GM Kim & GM Ji. Choi always warned about kicking above the waist due to the dangers and vulnerability in combat. There are however many very skilled kickers in both taekwondo and hapkido. I am not saying that learning proper kicking techniques has no value because learning proper kicking helps us to learn good balance and physical fitness.

With the many schools claiming to teach hapkido I warn the student looking for traditional hapkido training to do some research and ask questions to make sure the school you choose is what you are looking for.

My opinion is that if you find a skilled instructor that is humble and you enjoy the training they offer, you are doing very well. The character of the teacher you choose is always more important than what they teach in my humble opinion.
Hapkido has grown to a worldwide martial art with many practitioners all around the world. Even though hapkido has many different Associations and groups around the world many are starting to seek the authentic hapkido from Choi Young Sul and interest is growing as I write this.

Choi Doju-Nim always taught practical skills for self-defense and always warned against what today is called demonstration & sport hapkido.

Hapkido also has a special place in police and elite military teams around the world because of its highly efficient and effective techniques.

GM Lim Chae Kwan demonstrating technique on CM Todd Miller in Daegu South Korea.

Instructor Jeroen Malipaard from the Netherlands demonstrating hapkido technique.

5. Choi Young Sul

Founder of Hapkido – Choi Young Sul.

Much has been written about founder Choi Young Sul over the years and his legend is well known. I will try to keep this brief. Understand that I am writing about the stories I have been told by Choi's direct students through my 30 years of training and research, traveling to Korea many times in the pursuit thereof.

Choi was born during a turbulent time in Korea with the Japanese invasion of the Korean peninsula. Choi's birth year is said to be 1899. When Choi was very young he was kidnapped by a Japanese candy maker who was living in Korea. Choi was taken to Japan but did not like the candy maker and ran away to live on the streets. A Buddhist priest felt sympathy for the young boy and took him in to live with him. Choi would stare at the ancient paintings of warriors on the walls of the temple. After a while the priest asked Choi what he wanted to do with his life then Choi pointed to the painting of the warriors. The priest had a friend who was a skilled martial artist so he took Choi to meet this man Takeda Sokaku for his introduction. Takeda felt sorry for Choi's situation and saw a special quality in Choi, because of this he adopted Choi into his household. Many claim that Choi was only a house boy or servant of Takeda but Choi always claimed Takeda as his adopted father throughout his whole life.

Takeda Sokaku.

Many in the Japanese Daito Ryu circles claim Choi was never a student of Takeda but Choi Doju-Nim's skills told a different story.

One of the issues is that there are very few hapkido schools or associations that teach the pure hapkido that Choi taught.

Choi's hapkido was very deep with many techniques and principles. Choi taught his students to grab with full power and attack with strong intention in order to keep his hapkido practical and effective as a martial art! Some of the key points of Choi Doju-Nim's hapkido are:

Natural walking stance. Upright posture with the eyes looking forward and arms gently lowered to the side. Open hand with the thumb extended upward. Kicking and striking to very specific pressure points and not injuring students.

Most people who have been involved in the Korean martial arts for any amount of time know the name of Choi Young Sul as he was one of the most important figures in the martial arts of post WW2 Korea. There are some in the Korean martial arts community that have some bias against Choi due to the fact he was trained in Japan by a Japanese master.

When Choi first came to live with Takeda he was given duties to perform, one of them was to clean the training hall. Because of this he was always in the training area while Takeda was teaching. Choi was a very keen observer of Takeda's teaching and movement. After a long period (possibly 6 months to several years), while Takeda was not in the training hall, Choi saw several students struggling with a technique and offered them his help.

Takeda saw Choi demonstrating the technique at a very high level with the students. This so impressed Takeda because he had never taught that level of technique, from that time on Choi was Takeda's student until Takeda's death in 1943. Choi would tell accounts of his time in Japan to his students.

One of these stories was about the DRAJJ demonstration team that was invited to Hawaii in 1928. There was a giant professional wrestler who challenged the demonstration team and one by one due to his huge size and strength was able to defeat each of the members of Takeda's team except Choi! After defeating the other members Takeda looked at Choi and nodded his head signaling Choi to take care of this wrestler. Choi stood upright with both hands gently by his side, feet in a relaxed walking position when the wrestler grabbed his belt. Choi grabbed the wrestlers hand so he could not let go and stepped back and leaned back slightly to break his balance. He then kicked a pressure point at the wrestler's armpit and used his own knee to break the wrestlers elbow! This took Choi only about three seconds!

Choi Doju-Nim demonstrating short staff defense. Thank you GM Kim Jeong Yun for the historical picture.

After Takeda's death in 1943 Choi returned to Korea and settled in Daegu. Choi claims that the certificates given to him by Takeda were stolen at a train station when he returned to Korea. Some doubt this story but Choi never changed or altered his account of this and other stories about his time training under his teacher Takeda Sokaku in Japan.

Choi Doju-Nim demonstrating hapkido staff technique. Thank you GM Kim Jeong Yun for the historical picture.

After Choi returned to Korea there was not much for work so Choi sold rice cakes to save money to buy some pigs to raise. This is an important historical event as it led to Choi meeting his first student in Korea, Master Suh Bok Sup. Choi would go to the brewery that Suh's father owned to get the used rice and grain chaff to feed to his pigs. One day Choi was waiting in line and 5 thugs jumped in front of Choi in the line and Choi confronted the men! These men attempted to attack Choi but he defeated the 5 men easily! Suh Bok Sup saw the whole encounter from his 2nd story office window. Suh had never seen anything like Choi's fighting techniques before. He then called for Choi to be brought to his office. He asked Choi what kind of martial art he used to defeat the thugs. Choi asked Suh to grab his chest and Suh tried to grab his chest and Choi easily applied a painful armlock to Suh's arm and Suh (who held 2nd Dan in Yudo) tried to grab and throw Choi a second time but he easily threw Suh to the floor. Mr. Suh then asked Choi to teach him his martial art.

Master Suh Bok Sup demonstrating the armlock.

Choi started teaching Suh and these training sessions began as private training but as soon as people started hearing of Choi's skill they grew into a much larger group. Many famous hapkido practitioners trained with Choi during these early days of Hapkido. Most only trained for a very short time due the painful techniques. Some of these early students were GM Kim Yeong Jae, Master Ji Han Jae, Master Kim Mo Hyung & GM Kim Jeong Yoon (founder of Han Pul). This is just a small list of those that trained with Choi in the late 1940s and 1950s. Many came to Choi for training after they had already received high Dan grades from other teachers and each time the students could not make their techniques work on the regular every day students of Choi. This was disturbing to Choi because his former students did not have a good enough understanding to teach the key points that make his techniques work against unwilling opponents!

Toward the end of Choi's life he wanted to unite the growing number of Hapkido groups. He promoted GM Chang Chin Il to 9th Dan and gave him the responsibility of uniting Hapkido! As we see today this never happened. In my opinion the best we can do today is try as much as possible to get back to the authentic teachings of Hapkido's true founder, Choi Young Sul. We also need to as leaders in Hapkido not allow high Dan grades to be sold to the highest bidder without the consummate skill! We at the Jin Mu Kwan are trying to share the authentic Hapkido techniques that founder Choi taught and get back to the roots of Korean Hapkido which is Choi Young Sul and the skills he taught.

GM Chae Hung Jun demonstrating 2 person throw.

We all know of Choi's high skills but I feel it is very important for us to reflect on some of the other things Choi taught! Like humility and loyalty to our teachers. I was told a story in Korea by one of Choi's long time students about a seminar Choi taught in his old age. There were some young students who were trying to test Choi's skill! Choi even though he was old and not as strong as in his younger years he defeated the young men easily! He then rebuked them for their disrespectful attitude.

We as Martial artists must always keep in perspective that we are all human beings and have weaknesses. This should help us keep a healthy humility about ourselves. I can honestly say in my younger years I had too much arrogance and through time and training I realize Choi had great wisdom about the true spirit of martial arts training. A modest and respectful demeanor is the best way to carry ourselves as martial artists. Especially for those in leadership roles.

We need to train hard and consistently but more importantly we must show caring and love for others. We must help those who want help and those that do not want our help we just move on without anger or malice towards them. If we are going to leave hapkido in a better state than we found it. This attitude of humility, caring and loyalty to our teachers and students is mandatory!

Choi Young Sul demonstrating against multiple attackers, GM Kim Yeong Jae on right 1950's. Thank you GM Kim Jeong Yun for the historical picture.

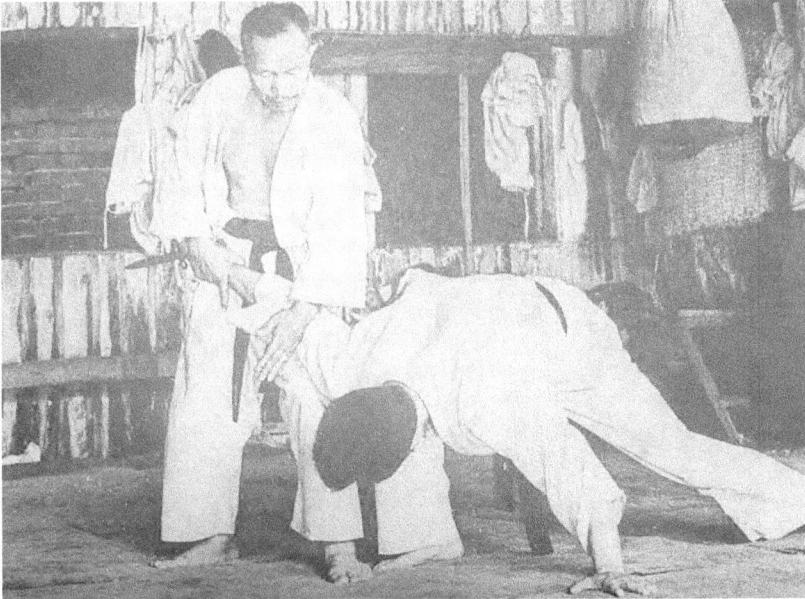

Choi Doju-Nim demonstrates knife defense in the 1950's. Thank you GM Kim Jeong Yun for the historical picture.

Choi Doju-Nim & Grandmaster Chae Hung Jun.

Birthday party for Choi Doju-Nim. GM Chae Hung Jun is on the right.

Choi Doju-Nim demonstrating against 3 attackers, Thank you GM Kim Jeong Yun for the historical picture.

Choi Doju-Nim in center of group photo at GM Kim Yeong Jae's hapkido school.

Choi Doju-Nim demonstrates on 2 attackers. Thank you to GM Kim Jeong Yun for the historical picture.

6. Michael Wollmershauser

GM Mike Wollmershauser in Korea, 1997.

Grandmaster Michael Wollmershauser holds a unique place in hapkido history as he was the only westerner to train with Founder Choi Young Sul in Korea. GM Wollmershauser's hapkido teacher GM Park Jung Hwan gave the recommendation for his introduction and training with Choi in 1979 during his trip to Daegu. GM Mike was the only known person to film founder Choi teaching and demonstrating hapkido techniques.

My training with Master Mike was important as I met many of the major leaders in the hapkido community such as GM Chang Jin Il, Master Suh Bok Sub, GM Chae Hung Jun, GM Lim Chae Kwan, Master Hal Whalen, Master Hwang In Shik and GM Chung Kee Tae & GM Chung Woo Duk. Just to name a few.

Master Suh Bok Sup, founder Choi's first Korean hapkido student.

I really value the time I spent with these Masters and Grandmasters. I remember during our interview with GM Chung Kee Tae, hearing how he taught the hapkido techniques found in the ITF encyclopedia written by General Choi Hong Hi. GM Chung KT and General Choi were friends and both lived in the Toronto area and met with each other regularly. GM Chung KT was also a very high ranking taekwondo grandmaster. GM Chung KT was a very kind man with a sparkle in his eyes! GM Chung KT had the scars of many years of hard training but was a very gentle and humble man.

Choi Young Sul seated, GM Chung Kee Tae standing & GM Chung's picture he signed for me during an interview GM Wollmershauser and I did with GM Chung in 1996.

GM Mike had a charisma that was infectious and he always loved to teach hapkido to anyone who was interested in learning. Master Mike ran the American Hapkido Association Summer Camp on Cape Cod for many years. These training camps were an excellent time of training and talking around the camp fire. Many people came to these camps over the years. GM Mike Wollmershauser made a significant contribution to hapkido by popularizing it during the 1980s and 90s. GM Mike also wrote many magazine articles on hapkido and its history.

7. Hapkido in Daegu, Korea

A Korean Master demonstrating his interpretation of hapkido on CM Todd Miller.

This school was first opened by this grandmaster in 1974 at the age of 30. This grandmaster started his hapkido training with GM Kim Yeong Jae, Choi's top student after many years of Tang Soo Do training. His Tang Soo Do training can be seen in his interpretation of hapkido by the wide, deep stances. This grandmaster broke the school into two groups, the main group was kumdo and kuhapdo. The smaller group was hapkido. This grandmaster trained in hapkido for a short time before his military service. He then opened his school after he was discharged from the military.

A Korean master demonstrating with CM Todd Miller & another American Master.

This Daegu, Korea school was the 2nd phase in my training. This was a great time for building relationships with people that I still train with today.

CM Todd Miller throwing Master Harvey Garod, Dover, NH.

This 2nd phase of training is where I met GM Chae Hung Jun and GM Lim Chae Kwan. Both are now members of the Jin Mu Kwan along with several other Masters from this hapkido school in Daegu. The training was very rigorous under

CM Todd Miller demonstrating a technique on his student Frank Weeks for a Korean master.

the direction of GM Lim Chae Kwan. These training sessions were difficult training. This is where I received the first Dan grade given to any foreigner in Kuhapdo/Iaido. I was also promoted to 5th Dan in hapkido by this school in 2002. This training helped me get another step closer to the authentic hapkido of Choi Young Sul.

Sightseeing at Korean hapkido summer camp in 1999. Front row: Todd & Michelle Miller, GM Chae Hung Jun, and others.

CM Todd Miller demonstrating a 2 person hapkido throw on Master Harvey Garod and Mr. Trevor Stone in 2005.

CM Todd Miller demonstrating a technique on his student in Korea.

8. GM Lim Chae Kwan and Jin Mu Kwan: The Authentic Martial School

GM Lim Chae Kwan, Hapkido 9th Dan.

The Jin Mu Kwan was founded by GM Lim Chae Kwan in 2007 after more than 40 years of experience in the hapkido of his teacher Choi Young Sul. GM Lim was taught directly by Choi Young Sul for 8 years and after Choi's passing GM Lim trained with many of Choi's most skilled students.

From right to left: GM Chae Hung Jun, GM Kim Yeong Jae and GM Lim Chae Kwan. GM Lim learned from both GM Chae and GM Kim.

GM Lim Chae Kwan teaching one of his early students.

The name of the Jin Mu Kwan is very important as its meaning actually tells what the Jin Mu Kwan teaches.

Jin Mu Kwan emblem.

Jin- Authentic & True
Mu- Martial
Kwan- School

GM Lim demonstrating the technique Choi used to defeat a professional wrestler during the 1928 Daito Ryu exhibition in Hawaii.

The goal of GM Lim and all members of the Jin Mu Kwan is to teach and share the authentic hapkido technology of Founder Choi Young Sul. I personally have trained with GM Lim for 22 years and know his ability and skill very well. GM Lim's focus has always been on using your Dan Jeon energy flowing through the wrist and fingertips.

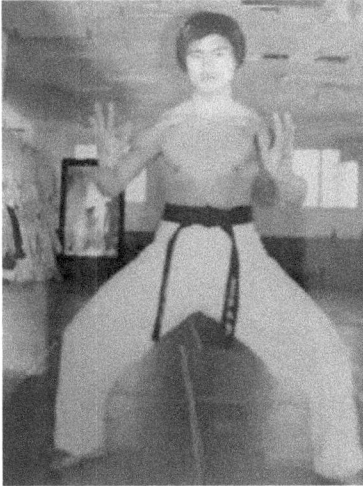

GM Lim practicing Dan Jeon breathing exercise as a young man in Korea.

This is the hapkido of Founder Choi. GM Lim had the great opportunity to take many private lessons with Choi Doju-Nim during his training with him. This has given him some valuable insights into Choi Doju-Nim's hapkido. GM Lim has made it his life's goal to do what he can to teach and share his vast experience and years of training in the authentic hapkido of Choi Young Sul so it is preserved for the next generation!

GM Lim demonstrating a short staff technique on CM Miller.

The following is an interview that I did with GM Lim in 2017 & 2018:

1. What is your training history? Who were some of your teachers?

GM Lim: I was born on February 15, 1962, the eldest son of my family. I came to Daegu to study in Elementary School in Jin Ju from age 11-13. I wanted to become a Taekwondo expert! I started learning Hapkido while in Middle School. I trained with Founder Choi Young Sul for 8 years and finally on 8/15/83, Choi Young Sul promoted me to 4th Dan Master of Hapkido!

After this I joined the Army for my Military service.

I have had a total of 7 Teachers in Hapkido and Iaido,

First of all I learned the most important skill from Hapkido Founder Choi Young Sul my first teacher.

Second, I learned the skill of kicking with GM Jun Jeong Pil.

Third, I learned advanced wrist technology from GM Lee, Jae Young.

Fourth, I learned the technology of clothing grab defense from GM Lee, Young Hee.

Fifth, I learned special offensive techniques for joint locking and throwing from GM Chae, Hung Jun

Sixth, I learned special self-protection techniques from GM Kim, Young Jae.

Seventh, I learned Iaido from grandmaster Komei Sekiguchi.

The reason for this is that there are a total 3680 techniques in Hapkido technology.
Nobody knew all the techniques of Choi Young Sul so I learned advanced techniques from the age of 14 directly from Choi and I learned from various teachers for 45 years from age 14 to learn as much of the Hapkido of Choi Young Sul that I could.
For many years, I have constantly learned new skills from various teachers. Therefore, I have specially advanced technology from 1st Dan to 9th Dan stage technology to share in Jin Mu Hapkido.

After many years of deep study into the Hapkido that Choi Young Sul taught.
I opened the Jin Mu Kwan in 2007 and now I am teaching Jin Mu Hapkido.

GM Lim Chae Kwan & GM Jun Jeong Pil.

Accomplishments

1. Korea Classical Martial Arts Association President
2. Korea Hapkido Master 4th Dan (Under Korea Hapkido Founder Choi Young Sul)
3. World Japan Iaido Association 6th Dan (Japan, Komei Sekiguchi).
4. Korea Taekwondo Master 4th Dan.
5. Tukong Mu Sool Master 6th Dan
6. Korean Hapkido Grandmaster 9th Dan.
7. Occupation: Daegu Fire Station 119 Special Rescue Team Leader
8. And From 1997 to 2007 I worked as Chief supervisor of the Hapkido Summer Camp seminars for USA and Europe, etc.

GM Lim Chae Kwan demonstrating Jin Mu Hapkido at Korean Hapkido demonstration.

2.What was your impressions of Choi Yong Sul?

2. Choi Young Sul was a very reticent person.
I could hardly believe my eyes when Founder Choi demonstrated his hapkido techniques. It was almost magical how easy and deliberate his movement was! Founder Choi had the eyes of a tiger that could pierce right through you! His hapkido was as strong as electricity!

If I suddenly met Choi in class, I called to him to check my technique and he always came over right away and I showed him a demonstration of the technique. Choi Young Sul's Hapkido was very high level Martial Arts technology.   For this reason I have studied diligently my whole life to become a skilled craftsman in Hapkido. As a matter of fact hapkido has a total of 3680 techniques according to Choi Young Sul. It takes 365 days a year and 10 years of practice if you practice it once a day!

Most importantly, he had scary and deadly skills.
I think what matters now is that our future is more important than the past. How we proceed is very important. You must keep this in mind.
Choi Young Sul's legend is already known to everybody.
I always respect him in my heart as he was my teacher.

GM Lim Chae Kwan practicing hapkido in the early 80's.

3. What was your early training like with Choi Yong Sul?

First of all, I greeted the opponent with respect by shaking hands and gave him an immediate bow, and he gave me a straight attack. He gave me a continuous attack with his fists. It was constant attack and defend with Choi. It is best practice to train your eyes. To look and see the intention of your attacker, this is what Choi Young Sul was highly skilled at!

Second, My younger brother and I worked for more than six months conditioning our wrists. My wrists were conditioned like a leather peel. This is excellent for saving your wrists from injury.

Third, Hapkido had no platform. However, I received a certificate when I finished cleaning the finishing touches and developed a curriculum with the key points of the real hapkido from Founder Choi.

Fourth, The training hall of Choi had 3 levels. The 1st floor was a basic training ground. The 2nd floor was a black belt training hall. The 3rd floor was for Grandmasters only!

On the 3rd floor No one could sneak a peek at anyone as it was not allowed!

GM Lim Chae Kwan demonstrating Jin Mu Hapkido.

4. What goals do you have for the Jin Mu hapkido Association in the future ?

Since I have learned Hapkido from childhood, Hapkido is the prop of my life.
It will lead to the development and dissemination of Jin Mu hapkido, the specialized spirit of the martial arts, which is the key to true Martial Arts practice.
I am going to complete the publication of a beginner's essay/book in English for beginners in hapkido.
I will make a beginner's video tape from White belt to 1st Dan, beginning to end.
And, of course, we will travel around the world to teach and nurture many students through seminars and demonstrations.

5. How has hapkido changed in Korea since your early years of training?

The principle of Hapkido is that the more you learn the more you want to study to learn more.

Hapkido posture is straight, and the eyes look straight, and the arms are gently lowered, and the legs are gently opened and the force or energy is flowing at the tip of the hand. These are the things I learned from Choi Young Sul.

Now hapkido is a complete jumble of many things. There has been a moving away from the true hapkido from Founder Choi and his teachings! It has been transformed considerably. In other words many things have been added to and taken away from the hapkido Choi taught.

6. What are some of the challenges in general for hapkido going forward?

We need to change it back to the true Choi Young Sul Style of hapkido.

It is important to unify hapkido technology with one thing, the technology of Choi Young Sul.
In Jin Mu Hapkido we are trying hard to promote hapkido with a lot of publicity and seminars and teaching in various areas. We are the future of hapkido. It is up to us to train, teach and share the wonderful art of hapkido with those who are interested in it!

7. What is your job outside of hapkido? How long have you been in this job?

I have a total of 27 years as a 119/911 fire fighter since 1990.
In my Fireman-related activities my department and I have also contributed to the saving of lives in many types of rescues such as Mountain, High building and water rescues.

8. You have a very interesting logo! Could you explain the meaning of the eagle, fist and the 119 in your logo?

First, a large circle represents space, and a small circle represents a person. After all, it's a big love affair we all have with life.

And the taegeuk symbol means a mix of people (mankind) under the sky.
This is the symbol of the national flag of South Korea taegeuki (Um/Yang, Blue and Red, equal and opposite).
And the eagle is the king of the sky who sees the heart with piercing and strong eyes.
Both fists represent defensive martial arts, not offensive martial arts.
And the 119/911 is to defend the week and helpless and to promote world peace.

GM Lim Chae Kwan & I are working on setting up Jin Mu study centers in many areas of the world to promote the correct practice of the hapkido handed down to us from the founder of hapkido Choi Young Sul. These study centers will continue to train and learn the high skills Choi Doju-Nim taught to GM Lim Chae Kwan.

GM Lim & CM Miller paying their respects to founder Choi Young Sul.

GM Lim Chae Kwan's 4th Dan certificate from founder Choi Young Sul.

The first Jin Mu Kwan Hapkido seminar in Dover, NH, 2006. Seated: CM Todd Miller, GM Lim Chae Kwan. Standing: Trevor Stone, Raurc Hoermann, Randy Lund, Master Harvey Garod, Bob Gauvin.

GM Chae Hung Jun demonstrating at Jin Mu Kwan hapkido demonstration 2009.

GM Lim demonstrating a wrist lock on CM Todd Miller in Korea. Notice the upright posture & stance GM Lim is using, 2018.

Jin Mu Kwan demonstration team in Korea, Front row from Left: Master Seo Dong Yoon, GM Chae Hung Jun, GM Lim Chae Kwan, CM Kang Deok Dil, unknown.

2019 Jin Mu Hapkido seminar in Concord, NH at NH Kicks Taekwondo & Family Fitness Center owned by GM Daniel Un Hak Jung.

GM Lim teaching Jamie Bowman at the Jin Mu International Seminar in NH 2019.

GM Lim teaching Master Chad Allen & Master Oniver Guerrero, 2019

GM Lim & his wife Mrs. Lee Sang Hee.

Jin Mu hapkido Netherlands group. This group is led by Instructor Jeroen Malipaard.

GM Lim with the Jin Mu Kwan Netherlands group in Korea. Left to right-Magreet Ouwens, Barry Kieboom, GM Lim Chae Kwan, Jeroen Malipaard & Wim Middelkoop.

9.Hapkido in America

Hapkido in America has gone through many changes and challenges over the years. It started with J.R. West the First American hapkido black belt from Mississippi who was promoted to 1st Dan in 1967 while stationed in Vietnam.

J.R. West hapkido 9th Dan and black belt since 1967.

Since that time many people have come and gone and hapkido has spread out all over America. Some of the important masters in the USA were Master Mike Wollmershauser who was the first and only American to train with Founder Choi in Korea.

Left picture: GM Hal Whalen demonstrating a cane technique. Right picture: GM Whalen throwing two of his students.

Left picture: GM Hal Whalen demonstrating on Master Fabian Duque. Right picture: GM Holcombe Thomas demonstrating on GM Whalen at J.R. West seminar in Mississippi.

I also want to mention grandmaster Hal Whalen from Boston who studied hapkido while stationed in Korea. GM Whalen has taught in the Boston area since the 1970's. The following was contributed by GM Hal Whalen.

"Having been involved in Hapkido for close to 42 years, I started my training in South Korea at a local Hapki-Dojang North of Seoul in what is considered the western corridor. I was the first Black Belt in the Boston area opening a dojang at a local YMCA for 20 years. The only other Hapkido was Mike Wollmershauser, a third dan under J. Park in Springfield, MA, whom I met at a local Karate Tournament in 1979. We were friends until his passing.

Through the years I have seen and witnessed a lot in the Hapkido world. Changes are sometimes good but why reinvent the wheel? For years before the internet those that knew, knew of each other and somehow it still spread with integrity and honor but times change as do motivation.

GM Won Kil Soo, GM Hal Whalen's teacher in Korea.

Having taught seminars around the country I found it less offending to students that trained with a different Kwan or Dojang where the variations may be slightly different a slight difference that is sometimes not noticeable to the untrained eye but often felt. I use the expression "Same car different driver" it makes them understand when I explain the theory how we all have the same car and we all drive differently because of our body's strengths and limitations. The basic principles of motion, body alignment, offsetting of your opponent's balance, have to be met before any technique will work. Keeping these concepts in mind the Same car different driver makes more sense."
Contributed by GM Hal Whalen

There are many other people that have made major contributions to hapkido that I will not mention due the nature of this book being an abbreviated overview. I only mention these people as I know them personally with the exception of GM West. I had the pleasure of speaking with GM West about the history of hapkido in the USA on a telephone interview.

Many Korean Masters and Grandmasters have immigrated to the USA. These Masters made great contributions to Hapkido's growth. Some of these men I will mention such as GM Bong Soo Han who was in the Billy Jack movies in the early 1970's , GM Park Jung Hwan who was Master Mike Wollmershauser's hapkido teacher. I also want to mention Michael Scarola who is a student of GM Park

Jung Hwan. Mr. Scarola tested for his blue belt with Choi Young Sul sitting on the testing board during Choi's visit to the USA. This was a great honor and only a very few have had this honor.

Michael Scarola & GM Park Jung Hwan.

GM Park was a direct student of Choi Young Sul and was promoted to 7th Dan by Choi. GM Park was a neighbor of Choi Doju-Nim and heard many stories of Choi keeping the neighborhood safe from gangsters. This was one of the reasons GM Park went to train with Choi Doju-Nim. GM Park came to the USA in 1971 and began teaching his craft to many American students.

Choi Young Sul & GM Park Jung Hwan.

GM Ho Soo Hwang started training with Choi at age 8 in 1952. GM Hwang immigrated to the USA in 1971 and started teaching in Connecticut. Several students of GM Hwang are GM David Ipacs and Master Chris Ipacs. They both started hapkido training under GM Hwang in 1971.

From left – GM David Ipacs, GM Ho Soo Hwang and Master Chris Ipacs.

GM Rim Jong Bae was also a student of Choi Young Sul and promoted to 7th Dan, he immigrated to the USA in 1973 and still lives in the Baltimore area.

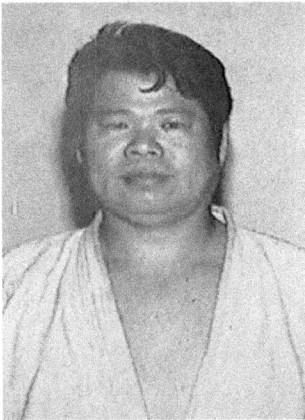

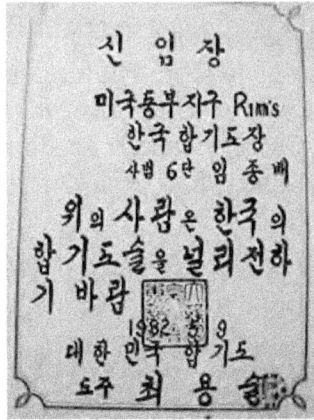

GM Rim Jong Bae, promoted to 7th Dan by Choi Young Sul. This Certificate was given to GM Rim by Choi in 1982 when he visited the USA.

There was also GM Chang Jin Il who lived in NYC. GM Chang was the first person to receive a 9th Dan from Choi Young Sul. GM Chang was also given the title of Doju (keeper of the way) by Choi.

GM Chang Chin Il.

Some claim that GM Chang was also promoted to 10th Dan. According to all of Choi's original students that I have talked with, they all agree that in Korean martial arts 9th dan is the highest level. So Choi would not have given a 10th dan as it would have gone against cultural norms of the time!

GM You Hyun Bae was probably one of the most influential teachers of hapkido in the Chicago area. GM You won many awards and championships in Korea before he moved to the USA such as National Champion of Korea in 1982 for – Best all around martial arts, Weapons, Self Defense & Best martial arts instructor of Korea hapkido association 1987. GM You is also an 8th dan in Jido Kwan taekwondo.

GM You Hyun Bae in front of his Chicago dojang in 1993 & GM You demonstrating a wrist throw on a student.

GM You Hyun Bae with a group of his students in Chicago.

GM Kim Myung Yong, the founder of the Jin Jung Kwan branch of hapkido moved to the USA in 1975, GM Rhodes has been a direct student of GM Kim for more than 20 years. GM Michael Rhodes was promoted to 9th Dan by GM Kim in 2018. GM Rhodes is also the Korea Hapkido Federation representative for the USA. GM Rhodes has been working to help keep hapkido relevant in the modern world by working to update the hapkido techniques for the threats we face today.

GM Kim Myung Yong & GM Michael Rhodes of the Jin Jung Kwan. GM Kim Promoted GM Rhodes to 9th Dan in 2018 and Headmaster of the Jin Jung Kwan.

GM Rhodes teaching at the Jin Jung Kwan USA Headquarters in Missouri and GM Rhodes with his son Logan Michael Rhodes.

GM Stuart Rosenberg is one of the highest ranking members of the World Sin Moo Hapkido Association under Sin Moo Hapkido creator GM Ji Han Jae. GM Rosenburg started training in hapkido in 1978 and was promoted to 9th Dan by GM Ji Han Jae in 2014 and was awarded his own Kwan called Sin Moo Anu Kwan.

GM Stuart Rosenburg, Sin Moo Hapkido 9th Dan. GM Ji Han Jae and GM Rosenburg working together.

GM Joseph Lumpkin started training in hapkido in 1971 and is now the headmaster of Shinsei hapkido. Shinsei hapkido is a Christian based program in Alabama.

Todd L. Miller

GM Joseph Lumpkin Headmaster of Shinsei Hapkido.

One of the challenges of hapkido in the USA is the promotion of unqualified masters. This problem makes it more difficult to find qualified masters and schools for training! This book will hopefully help those interested in hapkido training to research and learn about the differences between various schools and associations in order to make an educated choice.

Another challenge for hapkido is that some groups and organizations are losing the original hapkido technology. Through the lack of information and understanding they are adding bits and pieces of other martial arts into hapkido. This may not seem like a bad idea but the problem is that the addition of many other things may contradict the principles and philosophy of hapkido. This waters down the true essence of the authentic hapkido from Founder Choi Young Sul.

One of the positive things happening in the USA is that many of the senior masters and grandmasters are communicating with each other and encouraging each other. Many of these masters are from different groups and organizations. If hapkido is to survive I believe this kind of communication is essential to work together to help the hapkido community at large.

10. Methodology for the future generations

Videos can be a great tool to help a student learn in conjunction with a qualified master to train with and to bring forth the finer points that videos often miss. YouTube can be a good tool to see the many interpretations of hapkido. My only caution is that not everything on YouTube is done by skilled masters. There are some good videos out there as well, but it is important that people understand that anyone can post a video on YouTube and call it hapkido. Another failed method is bogus rank certification as a tool to fool the public. Some people even go from one organization to another looking for another promotion without putting the time in grade.

In traditional Korean martial arts 9th Dan is the highest Dan grade. To go along with this is the problem of many people not understanding the titles used in Korean martial arts. When I started training very few people claimed the title of grandmaster. This is an American title. In Korea if you own a martial arts school you are called Kwanjangnim. Today the term grandmaster is very common but it is not a traditional title. Another title that is misused is the title of doju or doju-nim. This title was used by Choi's students because he was the founder of Korean hapkido. The first was Choi Young Sul and the person he handed down the title of doju (keeper of the way) to GM Chang Jin Il. GM Chang died unexpectedly in 2018 and did not appoint a successor. I humbly assert there are no other doju's in the hapkido world. I also understand that some may disagree with my opinion.

Now more than ever the methodologies we use for teaching hapkido along with keeping our standards to a high level will determine the future of this very important martial art.

This has been one of the areas that both GM Lim and I have worked to develop some great modern ways of teaching the key principles of Jin Mu Hapkido/Authentic hapkido from Choi Young Sul. It is very important to use modern teaching methods and technologies to teach the authentic hapkido of Founder Choi. This has been very successful for Grandmaster Lim Chae Kwan in Korea and for myself in the USA. It is very important to continue to look for new and innovative ways to share our art.

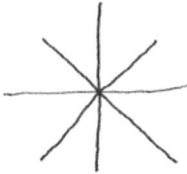

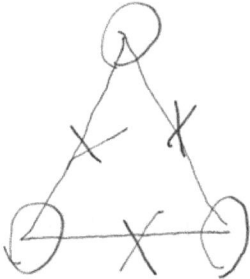

The top and middle diagrams are the angles we use in traditional hapkido, The bottom diagram shows the weak or dead angles we use for attack to break opponent's balance. These diagrams are from my personal notes and are very important for both teachers and students to study and understand.

We have taken into account the psychology of combat in our teaching method to add another dimension of understanding how the techniques work in real life situations. These teaching methods will help to teach the complete art of hapkido, that Founder Choi left to us, more effectively.

GM Lim has set up the Jin Mu Hapkido curriculum with advanced techniques introduced at the very beginning. He has also broken the techniques down so a new student can learn the basic movements and the advanced students can learn the higher level material in the same techniques. We still have a belt structure that teaches different concepts at each level in the curriculum similar to other martial arts systems. It is these kinds of innovations that will help keep hapkido interesting to all levels of training. These types of methodologies are key to keeping hapkido relevant in an ever changing world.

During the interviewing process for this book I talked with various leaders in hapkido from different schools and associations. Some common things that were discussed is that today in the hapkido world there are many unqualified masters, many arrogant practitioners that are very young and haven't stood the test of time. One quote that thought was very important for us all to consider from GM Joseph Lumpkin: *"The most important thing for us as teachers is to raise up students without our character flaws."* This brings to mind some of the benefits of traditional martial arts training that help us to develop our character. To rid ourselves of these character flaws such as arrogance, greed and selfishness. If we as leaders in hapkido set this as an important goal for ourselves first then our students will follow our lead. Hapkido has many practitioners around the world and human nature can only be changed one person at a time. If we talk about and live the importance of one's character on equal footing with good technical ability these changes will happen even if it is a slow process.

One of the most important things we can teach our students is the proper respect and courtesy between a student and teacher. A student should always give proper respect to his or her teacher and even more important is for a teacher to model this courtesy and respect to his or her students. These principles of courtesy and respect are probably the most important things we will share with our students and the world. In this same context the practice of sincere humility is very important for both masters and their students.

11. My work.

CM Miller at Choi Doju-Nim's Memorial site outside of Daegu, Korea.

My work in teaching the martial arts has always been to teach the traditional principles of martial arts. This includes the time tested skills that founder Choi taught. As I learned more of the authentic skills I had to make changes in what and how I taught. This was both difficult and enlightening for me as a teacher. I have always believed that the teachings passed on by Choi Doju-Nim were the most effective and powerful. The more I learn the more I believe this to be true. This is why from my first encounter with hapkido back in the 1970's until today I have always tried to learn and teach these techniques to the best of my ability.

CM Miller teaching Jin Mu Hapkido in 2008.

This approach to teaching martial arts has not changed in my 30 years as a martial arts instructor. My original goal was to teach traditional hapkido and taekwondo with a focus on the effective skills of self-defense.

CM Miller teaching at his school in Dover, NH, 1997.

I have always tried to give my students the best training possible. Challenging them to keep training even when they felt like quitting. Over the years I have taught taekwondo, aikido, hapkido, kuhapdo/iaido and bowie knife training. In this training I have also continued my research into the authentic hapkido taught by its true founder, Choi Young Sul.

I continue yearly trips to Daegu Korea for my own training with GM Lim Chae Kwan and learning more about the history of the art I love and have dedicated my life to help promote.

GM Lim demonstrating technique on CM Miller in Korea.

Over the last three years I have been working with people from many countries who have an interest in the authentic hapkido of founder Choi. We have scheduled many training camps and seminars to share the authentic hapkido from founder Choi with those masters and students that are interested in the root of all hapkido. My goal is to help share the great art of hapkido and build a strong following of dedicated hapkido practitioners who share in the goal of passing the authentic hapkido from Choi Doju-nim to the next generation.

Warriors Everywhere emblem.

To help in this I have started a new project with GM Luiz Miele from Brazil called Warriors Everywhere Productions. Our goal is to share our experience on martial arts from academies to companies. To use the best tools for any kind of person or groups, teaching martial arts in its true context, with movements, techniques or just simple exercises with reflections and thoughts that body and mind work together and can bring us health and balance everywhere in our daily lives.

CM Miller after a 3 goza cut at his Dover, NH dojang.

I have also been working with women's groups, children and people with disabilities, teaching self-defense strategies to help stop bullying and abuse. This has been very rewarding for me to see people gain confidence and realize that they have the power and abilities to not be a victim in life but to be victorious! The martial arts have so much to offer our world but many do not have enough time to devote themselves to learn a complete martial arts system. This is what got me started on developing a simplified curriculum to help everyone gain the knowledge and confidence to stay safe in our sometimes dangerous world.

CM Miller's 6th Dan certificate- 2008.

CM Miller's Chief Master Letter of Appointment from GM Lim Chae Kwan & Jin Mu Kwan.

Jin Mu Hapkido & Taekwondo Academy group picture with Lim Kwangjangnim and his wife Mrs. Lee Sang Hee.

CM Todd Miller with black belt Raurc Hoermann.

Standing: Master Harvey Garod, Bob Gauvin, Jim Kenney, Frank Weeks, Tom O'Hara, seated: CM Miller, Jeff Cardin, 2000.

Black belt instructors: Troy Pickering, CM Miller, Master Harvey Garod & Bob Gauvin, 2002.

12. Closing Thoughts.

CM Todd & Michelle Miller in Korea 2018 near Choi Doju-Nim's memorial site.

When I started this project I was 29 years old. I recorded everything that I learned, and when I heard anything about the history of hapkido and taekwondo I made notes and kept most of those notes over the years. I was always intrigued with the stories I heard about Choi Young Sul and when I started being involved with interviewing students that trained under Founder Choi I started to see similar accounts of the same stories. I took as many notes and then began my own interviews during my travels to South Korea with people who were lesser known students of Choi.

The truth is that Choi Doju-nim's skill was legendary but not many followed his teaching closely. Most of his students made changes due to their past experiences and previous training in arts such as tang soo do and taekwondo. And even though taekwondo and tang soo do are formidable martial arts, they are however very different from traditional hapkido as taught by Founder Choi.

It is my hope that after reading this book you will have a little more information about hapkido and some of the main people that have helped define the art. I am sure that you have figured out that my opinion is that Choi Young Sul is the founder of hapkido and some may disagree with this belief. It is very important for us to look for the things we can agree on and that opens up a respectful dialog for us to talk in a respectful way about areas we may disagree on.

Hapkido is a fantastic martial art with many choices for a diligent student to learn from. Whether you choose to learn the hapkido with high kicking or the traditional hapkido that founder Choi Young Sul taught. I believe that most forms of hapkido have something to offer depending on what you are interested in learning. Even though hapkido has many practitioners around the world we are still a relatively small group that has learned to withstand the pain of the many joint locks and throws again and again! If I could have one wish come true through this book I would hope that we as hapkido practitioners could learn to respect each other even if we disagree on some points. This will help us to have a meaningful conversation with each other and maybe we can all even learn some new things from each other if we try with open hearts and minds! It is my hope you have enjoyed the information presented in this book. May God bless you and your study of Korean martial arts.

Sincerely,

Todd Miller